ALL YOU KNIT ♥ IS LOVE ♥

First published in the United Kingdom in 2012 by
Collins & Brown
10 Southcombe Street
London
W14 0RA

An imprint of Anova Books Company Ltd

Design and text copyright © Collins & Brown 2012
Pattern and image copyright © Mint Publishing 2012

Distributed in the United States and Canada by
Sterling Publishing Co, 387 Park Avenue South,
New York, NY 10016-8810, USA

ISBN 978-1-90844-904-7

A CIP catalogue record for this book is available from
the British Library.

10 9 8 7 6 5 4 3 2 1

Reproduction by Rival Colour Ltd, UK
Printed and bound by 1010 Printing International Ltd, China

This book can be ordered direct from the publisher
at www.anovabooks.com

ALL YOU KNIT ♥ IS LOVE ♥

DEBBIE HARROLD

COLLINS & BROWN

CONTENTS

HOT STUFF

Materials

- ❤ **A yarn such as:** Patons Fab DK, approx. 68m/25g ball (100% acrylic)
  1 ball in Red 2323
  1 ball in Green 2319
- ❤ Pair of 3.75mm needles
- ❤ Tapestry needle
- ❤ Toy filling
- ❤ Short length of black yarn
- ❤ Two pairs of 5mm wiggle eyes
- ❤ Small pieces of black and pink felt
- ❤ PVA glue or a glue gun
- ❤ One red craft pipe cleaner

Tension

22 stitches and 30 rows over 10cm stocking stitch.

Body and head
(make 1 for each chilli)

Using 3.75mm needles and red yarn, cast on 3 sts.
Row 1 (RS): Knit.
Row 2: Purl.
Row 3: [Inc 1] twice, k1. (5 sts)
Work 3 rows in stocking stitch.

Row 7: Inc 1, knit to the last 2 sts, inc 1, k1. (7 sts)
Row 31: [K3, k2tog] 3 times, k2. (14 sts)
Row 32: Purl.
Row 33: [K2, k2tog] 3 times, k2. (9 sts)
Break off red yarn and join in green.
Row 34: [K1, k2tog] twice, k3. (7 sts)
Row 35: Purl.
Row 36: [K1, k2tog] twice, k1. (5 sts)
Row 37: P2tog, p1, p2tog. (3 sts)

Stem

Work a further 6 rows in garter stitch.
Break off yarn and thread through stitches on needle.
Draw tight and secure the end.

Making up

For the body and head, partially sew up the side seam, using mattress stitch or backstitch, insert stuffing and complete the seam.
Using picture as guide, embroider a mouth with the black yarn and, using glue, attach eyes and felt moustache and mouth to the head sections.
Using the pipe cleaners, make two arms with hands; then attach them to the base of each hot, little chilli.

HORNY DEVIL

Materials

- ❤ **A yarn such as:** Patons Fab DK, approx. 68m/25g ball (100% acrylic) I ball in Red 2323
- ❤ Pair of 3.75mm needles
- ❤ Tapestry needle
- ❤ Toy filling
- ❤ A small amount black yarn
- ❤ One pair of 10mm wiggle eyes
- ❤ Small pieces of red and white felt
- ❤ PVA glue or a glue gun
- ❤ Two large red craft pipe cleaners
- ❤ Craft wire

Body and head

Using 3.75mm needles and red yarn, cast on 6 sts.

Row 1 (RS): [Inc 1, knitwise] 6 times. (12 sts)

Row 2: Purl.

Row 3: [Inc 1, k1] 6 times. (18 sts)

Row 4: Purl.

Row 5: [Inc 1, k2] 6 times. (24 sts)

Row 6: Purl.

Row 7: [Inc 1, k3] 6 times. (30 sts)

Work 11 rows in stocking stitch.

Row 19: K2, [k2tog, k3] 5 times, k2tog, k1. (24 sts)

Row 20: Purl.

Row 21: K1, [k2tog, k2] 5 times, k2tog, k1. (18 sts)

Row 22: Purl.

Row 23: [K2tog, k1] 6 times. (12 sts)

Row 24: Purl.

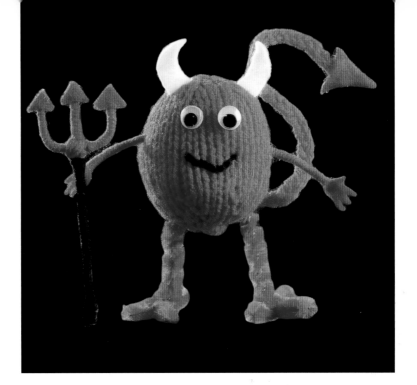

Row 25: [K2tog] 6 times. (6 sts)

Break off yarn and thread through stitches on needle.

Draw tight and secure the end.

Making up

For the body and head, partially sew up the side seam, using mattress stitch or backstitch, insert stuffing and complete the seam.

Using picture as guide, embroider the mouth with black yarn and, using glue, attach eyes.

From the white felt, cut out two horn shapes and, using glue, attach to the head.

Using the pipe cleaners, make two arms and two legs; then attach them to the base of the body.

Plait three strands of red wool with craft wire to make the tail and, using glue, attach to the body.

Using the pipe cleaners, make a trident shape, then wrap black yarn around the shaft and red yarn around each prong.

From red felt, cut out hands, small triangles for the points of the trident and a triangle for the tip of the tail, then, using glue, attach them to the little devil.

KISSES

Materials

- ❤ **A yarn such as:** Patons Fab DK, approx. 68m/25g ball (100% acrylic) 1 ball in Pink 2304
- ❤ Pair of 3.75mm needles
- ❤ Tapestry needle
- ❤ Toy filling
- ❤ Two pairs of 10mm wiggle eyes
- ❤ Short length of black yarn
- ❤ PVA glue or a glue gun
- ❤ One craft pipe cleaner

Tension

20 stitches and 29 rows over 10cm stocking stitch.

Body (make 1 for each pig)

Using 3.75mm needles and pink yarn, cast on 9 sts.
Row 1 (WS): Purl.
Row 2: [Inc 1] 9 times. (18 sts)
Row 3: Purl.
Row 4: [Inc 1] 18 times. (36 sts)
Work 25 rows in stocking stitch.
Row 30: [K2tog] 18 times. (18 sts)
Row 31: [P2tog] 9 times. (9 sts)
Row 32: K1, [k2tog] 4 times. (5 sts)
Break off yarn and thread through stitches on needle.
Draw tight and secure the end.

Head (make 1 for each pig)

Using 3.75mm needles and pink yarn, cast on 5 sts.
Row 1 (WS): Purl.
Row 2: [Inc 1] 5 times. (10 sts)

Row 3: Purl.
Row 4: [Inc 1] 10 times. (20 sts)
Work 13 rows in stocking stitch.
Row 30: [K2tog] 10 times. (10 sts)
Row 31: [P2tog] 5 times. (5 sts)
Row 32: K1, [k2tog] 4 times. (5 sts)
Break off yarn and thread through stitches on needle.
Draw tight and secure the end.

Nose (make 1 for each pig)

Using 3.75mm needles and pink yarn, cast on 3 sts.
Row 1 (WS): Knit.
Row 2: [Inc 1 knitwise] 3 times. (6 sts)
Row 3: [Inc 1 knitwise] 6 times. (12 sts)
Work 2 rows in garter stitch.
Row 6: [K2tog] 6 times. (6 sts)
Row 7: [K2tog] 3 times. (3 sts)
Break off yarn and thread through stitches on needle.
Draw tight and secure the end.

Ears (make 2 for each pig)

Using 3.75mm needles and pink yarn, cast on 6 sts.
Work 3 rows in garter stitch.
Break off yarn and thread through stitches on needle.
Draw tight and secure the end.

Legs (make 4 for each pig)

Using 3.75mm needles and pink yarn, cast on 5 sts.
Work 8 rows in stocking stitch.
Cast off.

Tail (make 1 for each pig)

Using 3.75mm needles and pink yarn, cast on 4 sts.
Work 11 rows in stocking stitch.
Cast off.

Making up

For the body and head, partially sew up side seam, using mattress stitch or backstitch, insert stuffing and complete the seam.

Using picture as guide and matching yarn, attach the nose and ears and, using glue, attach the eyes. Embroider nostrils using satin stitch.

For the legs and tail, cut a length of pipe cleaner to match the length of the knitted piece, sew up the seam around the pipe cleaner, shape and attach to the body.

CUDDLE BUNNY

Materials

- ♥ **A yarn such as:** Patons Fab DK, approx. 274m/100g ball (100% acrylic) 1 ball in Beige (B) 2308 Patons Fab DK, approx. 68m/25g ball (100% acrylic) 1 ball in White (W) 2306 1 ball in Pink 2304
- ♥ Pair of 3.75mm needles
- ♡ Tapestry needle
- ♥ Toy filling

Tension

22 stitches and 30 rows over 10cm stocking stitch.

SMALLER BUNNY

Body and head

Using 3.75mm needles and beige yarn, cast on 12 sts.
Row 1 (WS): Purl.
Row 2: [Inc 1, k1] 6 times. (18 sts)
Row 3: Purl.
Row 4: [Inc 1, k1] 9 times. (27 sts)
Work 10 rows in stocking stitch.
Row 15: P13, p2tog, p12. (26 sts)
In foll row, join white (W) and weave beige (B) across the back of the work.
Row 16: K11B, k4W, k11B.
Row 17: P10B, k6W, k10B.
Row 18: K9B, k8W, k9B.
Row 19: P8B, k10W, k8B.
Row 20: K7B, k12W, k7B.

Row 21: P3B, p2togB, p1B, p3W, p2togW, p4W, p2togW, p4B, p2togB, p1B. (22 sts)
Row 22: K1B, k2togB, k3B, k2togW, k3W, k2togW, k3W, k2B, k2togB, k2B. (18 sts)
Row 23: P2B, p2togB, p1B, p1W, p2togW, p2W, p2togW, p1W, p2B, p2togB, p1B. (14 sts)
Break off white yarn.
Row 24: [Inc 1, k1] 7 times. (21 sts)
Work 9 rows in stocking stitch.
Row 34: [K1, k2tog] 7 times. (14 sts)
Row 35: [P2tog] 7 times. (7 sts)
Break off yarn and thread through stitches on needle.
Draw tight and secure the end.

Arms (make 2)

Using 3.75mm needles and beige yarn, cast on 4 sts.
Row 1 (WS): Purl.
Row 2: [Inc 1] 4 times. (8 sts)
Work 9 rows in stocking stitch.
Row 12: [K2tog] 4 times. (4 sts)
Break off yarn and thread through stitches on needle.
Draw tight and secure the end.

Feet (make 2)

Using 3.75mm needles and beige yarn, cast on 6 sts.
Row 1 (WS): Purl.
Row 2: [Inc 1] 6 times. (12 sts)
Work 9 rows in stocking stitch.
Row 12: [K2tog] 6 times. (6 sts)

Row 13: [K2tog] 3 times. (3 sts)
Break off yarn and thread through stitches on needle.
Draw tight and secure the end.

Tail

Using 3.75mm needles and white yarn, cast on 3 sts.
Row 1 (WS): Knit.
Row 2: [Inc 1 knitwise] 3 times. (6 sts)
Row 3: [Inc 1 knitwise] 6 times. (12 sts)
Work 2 rows in garter stitch.
Row 6: [K2tog] 6 times. (6 sts)
Row 7: [K2tog] 3 times. (3 sts)
Break off yarn and thread through stitches on needle.
Draw tight and secure the end.

Outer ears (make 2)

Using 3.75mm needles and beige yarn, cast on 3 sts.
Row 1 (RS): [Inc 1] twice k1. (5 sts)
Row 2: Inc 1, p2, inc 1, p1. (7 sts)
Work 4 rows in stocking stitch.
Row 7: K2tog, k3, k2tog. (5 sts)
Work 3 rows in stocking stitch.
Row 11: K2tog, k1, k2tog. (3 sts)
Work 3 rows in stocking stitch.
Cast off.

Inner ears (make 2)

Using 3.75mm needles and pink yarn, cast on 3 sts.
Work as for Outer ears.

Making up

For the body and head, partially sew up side seam, using mattress stitch or backstitch, insert stuffing and complete the seam.

For the arms and feet, with the stocking stitch side facing outwards, fold the each piece in half and sew together around the outer edge.

For ears, with the stocking stitch side facing outwards, sew the two pieces together, using mattress stitch or backstitch, around the edge.

Using picture as guide, embroider the mouth and nose using backstitch, eyes using satin stitch and make whiskers. Using matching yarn, attach arms, feet, tail and ears.

LARGER BUNNY

Body and head

Using 3.75mm needles and beige yarn, cast on 12 sts.

Row 1 (WS): Purl.

Row 2: [Inc 1, k1] 6 times. (18 sts)

Row 3: Purl.

Row 4: [Inc 1, k1] 9 times. (27 sts)

Row 5: Purl.

Row 6: [Inc 1, k2] 9 times. (36 sts)

Work 14 rows in stocking stitch.

Row 21: P17, p2tog, p17. (35 sts)

In foll row, join white (W) and weave beige (B) across the back of the work.

Row 22: K17B, k1W, k17B.

Row 23: P16B, k3W, k16B.

Row 24: K15B, k5W, k15B.

Row 25: P3B, [p2togB, p3B] twice, p1B, p7W, p1B, [p2togB, p3B] twice, p3B. (31 sts)

Row 26: K2B, [k2togB, k2B] twice, k1B, k2togW, k5W, k2togW, k1B, [k2togB, k2B] twice, k2B. (25 sts)

Row 27: P2B, [p2togB, p1B] twice, p1W, p2togW, p3W, p2togW, p1W, [p2togB, p1B] twice, p2B. (19 sts)

Break off white yarn.

Row 28: K1, [inc 1, k1] 9 times. (28 sts)

Work 15 rows in stocking stitch.

Row 44: K1, [k2tog, k2] 6 times, k2tog, k1. (21 sts)

Row 45: Purl.

Row 46: [K1, k2tog] 7 times. (14 sts)

Row 47: [P2tog] 7 times. (7 sts)

Break off yarn and thread through stitches on needle.

Draw tight and secure the end.

Arms (make 2)

Using 3.75mm needles and beige yarn, cast on 8 sts.

Row 1 (WS): Purl.

Row 2: [Inc 1] 4 times. (8 sts)

Work 9 rows in stocking stitch.

Row 12: [K2tog] 4 times. (4 sts)

Break off yarn and thread through stitches on needle.

Draw tight and secure the end.

Feet (make 2)

Using 3.75mm needles and beige yarn, cast on 10 sts.

Row 1 (WS): Purl.

Row 2: [Inc 1] 6 times. (12 sts)

Work 9 rows in stocking stitch.

Row 12: [K2tog] 6 times. (6 sts)

Row 13: [K2tog] 3 times. (3 sts)

Break off yarn and thread through stitches on needle.

Draw tight and secure the end.

Tail

Using 3.75mm needles and white yarn, cast on 4 sts.

Row 1 (WS): Knit.

Row 2: [Inc 1, knitwise] 4 times. (8 sts)

Row 3: [Inc 1, knitwise] 8 times. (16 sts)

Work 4 rows in garter stitch.

Row 8: [K2tog] 8 times. (8 sts)

Row 9: [K2tog] 4 times. (4 sts)

Break off yarn and thread through stitches on needle.

Draw tight and secure the end.

Outer ears (make 2)

Using 3.75mm needles and beige yarn, cast on 3 sts.

Row 1 (RS): [Inc 1] twice, k1. (5 sts)

Row 2: Inc 1, p2, inc 1, p1. (7 sts)

Row 3: Inc 1, k4, inc 1, k1. (9 sts)

Work 7 rows in stocking stitch.

Row 11: K1, k2tog, k3, k2tog, k1. (7 sts)

Work 3 rows in stocking stitch.

Row 15: K1, k2tog, k1, k2tog, k1. (5 sts)

Work 3 rows in stocking stitch.

Row 19: K2tog, k1, k2tog. (3 sts)

Work 3 rows in stocking stitch.

Cast off.

Inner ears (make 2)

Using 3.75mm needles and pink yarn, cast on 3 sts.

Work as for Outer ears.

Making up

For the body and head, partially sew up side seam, using mattress stitch or backstitch, insert stuffing and complete the seam.

For the arms and feet, with the stocking stitch side facing outwards, fold the each piece in half and sew together around the outer edge.

For ears, with the stocking stitch side facing outwards, sew the two pieces together, using mattress stitch or backstitch, around the edge.

Using picture as guide, embroider the mouth and nose using backstitch, eyes using satin stitch and make whiskers.

Using matching yarn, attach arms, feet, tail and ears.

PERFECT CATCH

Materials

- ❤ **A yarn such as:** Patons Fab DK, approx. 68m/25g ball (100% acrylic)
  1 ball in Yellow 2323
  1 ball in Blue 2321
- ❤ Pair of 3.75mm needles
- ❤ Stitch holder
- ❤ Tapestry needle
- ❤ Toy filling
- ❤ Short length of black yarn
- ❤ Two pairs of 10mm wiggle eyes
- ❤ PVA glue or a glue gun
- ❤ Two thick red craft pipe cleaners

Tension

21 stitches and 30 rows over 10cm stocking stitch.

YELLOW FISH

Head and body (make 2)

Using 3.75mm needles and yellow yarn, cast on 4 sts.

Row 1 (WS): Purl.
Row 2: Inc 1, knit to last 2 sts, inc 1, k1. (6 sts)
Row 3: Inc 1, purl to last 2 sts, inc 1, k1. (8 sts)
Row 4: Inc 1, knit to last 2 sts, inc 1, k1. (10 sts)
Row 5: Purl.
Repeat last 2 rows 3 times more. (16 sts)
Work 10 rows in stocking stitch.
Row 22: K1, sl1, k1 psso, knit to last 3 sts, k2tog, k1. (14 sts)

Row 23: Purl.
Repeat last 2 rows 4 times more. (6 sts)
Row 32: K1, sl1, k1 psso, k2tog, k1. (4 sts)
Row 33: Purl.
Row 34: Cast on 4 stitches knit to end. (8 sts)
Row 35: Cast on 4 stitches purl to end. (12 sts)

Right tail lobe

Row 36: Inc 1, k5, turn transfer the rem 6 sts onto a stitch holder. (7 sts)
Row 37: P5, inc 1, p1. (8 sts)
Row 38: Inc 1, k6. (9 sts)
Row 39: P1, p2tog, purl to last 3 sts, p2togtbl, p1. (7 sts)
Row 40: K1, sl1, k1, psso, k1, k2tog, k1. (5 sts)
Row 41: P2tog, p1, p2togtbl. (3 sts)
Cast off.

Left tail lobe

Transfer stitches from stitch holder onto the needle and rejoin yarn.
Row 36: K4, inc 1, k1. (7 sts)
Row 37: Inc 1, p6. (8 sts)
Row 38: K6, inc 1, k1. (9 sts)
Row 39: P2tog, purl to last 2 sts, p2togtbl. (7 sts)
Row 40: Sl1, k1, psso, knit to last 2 sts, k2tog. (5 sts)
Row 41: P2tog, p1, p2togtbl. (3 sts)
Cast off.

Side fins (make 4)

Using 3.75mm needles and yellow yarn, cast on 5 sts.
Row 1 (RS): Knit.
Row 2: Purl.
Row 3: Sl1, k1, psso, k1, k2tog. (3 sts)
Work 5 rows in stocking stitch.
Row 9: [Inc 1] twice, k1. (5 sts)
Row 10: Purl.
Row 11: Knit.
Cast off.

Top fin

Using 3.75mm needles and yellow yarn, cast on 24 sts.
Row 1 (RS): [K1, p1] to end.
Repeat last row twice more.
Row 4: Sl1, k2tog, psso, [p1, k1] to last 3 sts, sl1, k2tog, psso. (20 sts)
Repeat last row 3 times more. (8 sts)
Cast off in rib.

Making up

For the head and body, partially sew the two pieces together using mattress stitch or backstitch, insert stuffing and complete the seam.

For the side fins, with the reverse stocking stitch side facing outwards, fold in half, cast-on edge to cast-off edge, and sew together around the outer edge.

Using picture as guide and matching yarn, attach the side fins to the side of the body and the top fin; embroider the mouth using backstitch; using glue, attach the eyes.

BLUE FISH

Head and body (make 2)

Using 3.75mm needles and blue yarn, cast on 4 sts.
Row 1 (WS): Purl.
Row 2: Inc 1, knit to last 2 sts, inc 1, k1. (6 sts)
Row 3: Inc 1, purl to last 2 sts, inc 1, p1. (8 sts)
Repeat last 2 rows once more. (12 sts)
Row 6: Inc 1, knit to last 2 sts, inc 1, k1. (14 sts)
Work 4 rows in stocking stitch.
Break off blue yarn and join in yellow.
Work 2 rows in stocking stitch.
Break off yellow yarn and join in blue.
Work 2 rows in stocking stitch.
Row 15: K1, sl1, k1, psso, k8, k2tog, k1. (12 sts)
Row 16: Purl.
Break off blue yarn and join in yellow.

Row 17: K1, sl1, k1, psso, k6, k2tog, k1. (10 sts)
Row 18: Purl.
Break off yellow yarn and join in blue.
Row 19: K1, sl1, k1, psso, k4, k2tog, k1. (8 sts)
Row 20: Purl.
Row 21: K1, sl1, k1, psso, k2, k2tog, k1. (6 sts)
Row 22: Purl.
Row 23: K1, sl1, k1, psso, k2tog, k1. (4 sts)
Row 24: Purl.
Row 25: Inc 1, knit to last 2 sts, inc 1, k1. (6 sts)
Row 26: Inc 1, purl to last 2 sts, inc 1, p1. (8 sts)
Repeat last 2 rows twice more. (12 sts)
Row 31: Inc 1, k3, sl1, k2tog, psso, k3, inc 1, k1. (12 sts)
Row 32: Inc 1, purl to last 2 sts, inc 1, p1. (14 sts)
Row 33: Inc 1, k4, sl1, k2tog, psso, k4, inc 1, k1. (14 sts)
Cast off.

Side fins (make 4)

Using 3.75mm needles and blue yarn, cast on 2 sts.
Row 1 (RS): Inc 1, knit to last 2 sts, inc 1, k1. (4 sts)
Row 2: Purl.
Repeat last 2 rows once more. (6 sts)
Work 2 rows in stocking stitch.
Row 7: K1, sl1, k1, psso, k2tog, k1. (4 sts)
Row 8: Purl.
Row 9: Sl1, k1, psso, k2tog. (2 sts)
Row 10: Purl.
Cast off.

Top fin

Using 3.75mm needles and blue yarn, cast on 5 sts.
Row 1 (WS): Purl.
Row 2: [Inc 1 knitwise] twice, k1, [inc 1 knitwise] twice. (9 sts)
Row 3: Purl.
Row 4: [Inc 1 knitwise] twice, k5, [inc 1 knitwise] twice. (13 sts)
Row 5: Purl.
Cast off.

Making up

For the head and body, partially sew the two pieces together using mattress stitch or backstitch, insert stuffing and complete the seam.

For the side fins, with the reverse stocking stitch side facing outwards, fold in half, cast-on edge to cast-off edge, and sew together around the outer edge.

Using picture as guide and matching yarn, attach the side fins and top fin; embroider fin detail using straight stitch and the mouth using backstitch; using glue, attach the eyes.

CUTE CHICK

Materials

- ❤ **A yarn such as:** Patons Fab DK, approx. 68m/25g ball (100% acrylic)
  1 ball in Blue 2315
  1 ball in Yellow 2305
  1 ball in Cream 2307
- ♡ Pair of 3.75mm needles
- ♡ Tapestry needle
- ❤ Toy filling
- ♡ One pair of 10mm wiggle eyes
- ♡ PVA glue or a glue gun

Tension

21 stitches and 30 rows over 10cm stocking stitch.

Body and head

Using 3.75mm needles and blue yarn, cast on 12 sts.
Row 1 (RS): [Inc 1 knitwise] 12 times. (24 sts)
Row 2: Purl.
Row 3: [Inc 1, k1] 24 times. (48 sts)
Row 4: Purl.
Work 12 rows in stocking stitch.
Row 17: K2 [k2tog, k4] 7 times, k2tog, k2. (40 sts)
Row 18: Purl.
Row 19: K1 [k2tog, k3] 7 times k2tog, k2. (32 sts)
Row 20: Purl.
Row 21: [K2tog, k2] 8 times. (24 sts)
Row 22: Purl.
Row 23: [Inc 1, k1] 24 times. (48 sts)
Row 24: Purl.
Work 10 rows in stocking stitch.

Row 35: [K2tog] to end. (24 sts)
Row 36: [P2tog] to end. (12 sts)
Row 37: [K2tog] to end. (6 sts)
Break off yarn and thread through stitches on needle.
Draw tight and secure the end.

Base

Using 3.75mm needles and cream yarn, cast on 8 sts.
Row 1 and each alternate row (WS): Purl.
Row 2: [Inc 1] 8 times (16 sts)
Row 4: [Inc 1, k1] 8 times. (24 sts)
Row 6: [Inc 1, k2] 8 times. (32 sts)
Row 8: [Inc 1, k3] 8 times. (40 sts)
Row 9: Purl.
Cast off.

Wings (make 2)

Using 3.75mm needles and blue yarn, cast on 3 sts.
Row 1 (WS): Purl.
Row 2: [Inc 1] twice, k1. (5 sts)
Row 3: Inc 1, p2, inc 1, p1. (7 sts)
Row 4: Inc 1, k4, inc 1, k1. (9 sts)
Row 3: Inc 1, p6, inc 1, p1. (11 sts)
Work 8 rows in stocking stitch.
Cast off.

Tail

Using 3.75mm needles and blue yarn, cast on 3 sts.
Row 1 (WS): Purl.
Row 2: Inc 1, knit to last 2 sts, inc 1, k1. (5 sts)

Repeat last 2 rows twice more. (9 sts)
Work 5 rows in stocking stitch.
Row 10: [K2, psso] 4 times, k1. (5 sts)
Row 11: P1, cast on 1 st [p2, cast on 1 st] 3 times. (9 sts)
Work 4 rows in stocking stitch.
Row 16: Sl1, k1, psso, knit to last 2 sts, k2tog. (7 sts)
Row 17: Purl.
Repeat last 2 rows twice more. (3 sts)
Row 22. Knit.
Cast off.

Beak

Using 3.75mm needles and yellow yarn, cast on 3 sts.
Row 1 (WS): Purl.
Row 2: [Inc 1] twice, k1. (5 sts)
Row 3: Inc 1, p2, inc 1, p1. (7 sts)
Work 8 rows in stocking stitch.
Row 12: K1, k2togtbl, k1, k2tog, k1. (5 sts)
Row 13: P2tog, p1, p2togtbl. (3 sts)
Row 14: Knit.
Cast off.

Making up

For the body and head, partially sew up side seam, using mattress stitch or backstitch, insert stuffing and complete the seam.

Stitch the base to the bottom of the body.

For the wings, with the stocking stitch side facing outwards, fold each wing in half lengthways and sew together around the outer edge.

For the tail and beak, with the stocking stitch side facing outwards, fold in half, cast-on edge to cast-off edge, and sew together around the outer edge.

Using picture as guide and matching yarn, attach the wings, beak and tail and, using glue, attach the eyes.

BEE MINE

Materials

- ♥ **A yarn such as:** Patons Fab DK, approx. 68m/25g ball (100% acrylic)
  1 ball in Yellow 2305
  1 ball in Black 2311
- ♥ Pair of 3.75mm needles
- ♥ Tapestry needle
- ♥ Toy filling
- ♥ Short length of red yarn
- ♥ Two pairs of 5mm wiggle eyes
- ♥ Scrap of white fine net
- ♥ PVA glue or a glue gun

Tension

22 stitches and 30 rows over 10cm stocking stitch.

Body and head
(make 1 for each bee)

Using 3.75mm needles and black yarn, cast on 8 sts.
Row 1 (WS): Purl.
Row 2: [Inc 1] 8 times. (16 sts)
Row 3: Purl.
Row 4: [Inc 1] 16 times. (32 sts)
Work 6 rows in stocking stitch.
Break off black yarn, join in yellow yarn.
Work 4 rows in stocking stitch.
Break off yellow yarn, join in black yarn.
Work 4 rows in stocking stitch.
Break off black yarn, join in yellow yarn.
Work 4 rows in stocking stitch.
Break off yellow yarn, join in black yarn.
Work 3 rows in stocking stitch.
Row 26: [K2tog] 16 times. (16 sts)
Row 27: [P2tog] 8 times. (8 sts)

Row 28: [K2tog] 4 times. (4 sts)
Break off yarn and thread through stitches on needle.
Draw tight and secure the end.

Making up

For the body and head, partially sew up side seam, using mattress stitch or backstitch, insert stuffing and complete the seam.
Using picture as guide, embroider the mouth using backstitch and, using glue, attach the eyes.
For the wings, cut from the fine net two pairs of rounded rectangles, 3cm x 7cm, pinch and gather each pair and attach to the back of the bee.

HA PEA VALENTINE'S

Materials

- **A yarn such as:** Patons Fab DK, approx. 68m/25g ball (100% acrylic) I ball in Green 2317
- Pair of 3.75mm needles
- Tapestry needle
- Toy filling
- Two pairs of 10mm wiggle eyes
- Small pieces of red and pink felt
- PVA glue or a glue gun
- A short length of 12mm organza ribbon

Body and head (make 1 for each pea)

Using 3.75mm needles and green yarn, cast on 6 sts.

Row 1 (RS): [Inc 1, knitwise] 6 times. (12 sts)

Row 2: Purl.

Row 3: [Inc 1, k1] 6 times. (18 sts)

Row 4: Purl.

Row 5: [Inc 1, k2] 6 times. (24 sts)

Work 9 rows in stocking stitch.

Row 15: K1 [k2tog, k2] 5 times, k2tog, k1. (18 sts)

Row 16: Purl.

Row 17: [K2tog, k1] 6 times. (12 sts)

Row 18: Purl.

Row 19: [K2tog] 6 times. (6 sts)

Break off yarn and thread through stitches on needle.

Draw tight and secure the end.

Making up

For the body and head, partially sew up side seam, using mattress stitch or backstitch, insert stuffing and complete the seam.

Using picture as guide cut out two mouth shapes from the felt and, using glue, attach eyes and mouths to each head.

Using the organza ribbon, tie a bow and attach to one of the sweet peas.

THINKING OF EWE

Materials

- **A yarn such as:** Wendy Mode Aran, approx. 200m/100g ball (50% acrylic, 50% wool)
  1 ball in White 201
  1 ball in Black 220
- Pair of 4.5mm needles
- Tapestry needle
- Toy filling
- Short length of white yarn
- Two pairs of 10mm wiggle eyes
- PVA glue or a glue gun
- One craft pipe cleaner

Body and head

Using 4.5mm needles and white yarn, cast on 7 sts.
Row 1 (RS): Knit.
Row 2: [Inc 1 knitwise] 7 times. (14 sts)
Row 4: [Inc 1 knitwise] 14 times. (28 sts)
Work 14 rows in garter stitch.
Row 19: K1, k2togtbl, knit to the last 3 sts, k2tog, k1. (26 sts)
Repeat the last row 6 times more. (14 sts)
Break off cream yarn, join black yarn.
Work 6 rows in stocking stitch.
Row 31: K1, [k2tog, k1] 4 times, k1. (10 sts)
Row 32: Purl.
Row 33: [K1, k2tog] 3 times, k1. (7 sts)
Row 34: Purl.
Row 35: [K2tog] 3 times, k1. (4 sts)
Break off yarn and thread through stitches on needle.
Draw tight and secure the end.

Tail

Using 4.5mm needles and cream yarn, cast on 4 sts.
Work 10 rows in stocking stitch.
Cast off.

Ears (male 2)

Using 4.5mm needles and black yarn, cast on 4 sts.
Work 10 rows in garter stitch.
Break off yarn and thread through stitches on needle.
Draw tight and secure the end.

Legs (make 4)

Using 4.5mm needles and black yarn, cast on 4 sts.
Work 8 rows in stocking stitch.
Cast off.

Making up

For the body and head, partially sew up side seam, using mattress stitch or backstitch, insert stuffing and complete the seam.
Using picture as guide, attach ears and tail then embroider nose using satin stitch; using glue, attach the eyes.
For the legs, cut a length of pipe cleaner to match the length of the piece, sew up the seam around the pipe cleaner, shape and attach to the body.

YOU'RE P-P-P-PERFECT

Materials

- ❤ **A yarn such as:** Sirdar Toytime DK Bonus, approx. 70m/25g ball (100% acrylic)
  1 ball in Black 965
  1 ball in White 961
  1 ball in Orange 981
- ❤ Pair of 3.75mm needles
- ❤ Stitch holder
- ❤ Tapestry needle
- ❤ Toy filling
- ❤ Two pairs of 10mm wiggle eyes
- ❤ Piece of thin card
- ❤ PVA glue or a glue gun
- ❤ One miniature bowtie

Tension

22 stitches and 26 rows over 10cm stocking stitch.

Body and head

Using 3.75mm needles and black yarn, cast on 12 sts.
Row 1 (WS): Purl.
Row 2: [Inc 1] 12 times. (24 sts)
Row 3: Purl.
Row 4: [Inc 1, k1] 12 times. (36 sts)
Work 25 rows in stocking stitch.
Row 30: [K1, k2tog] 12 times. (24 sts)
Work 11 rows in stocking stitch.
Row 42: [K2tog] 12 times. (12 sts)
Row 43: [P2tog] 6 times. (6 sts)
Break off yarn and thread through stitches on needle.
Draw tight and secure the end.

White bib

Using 3.75mm needles and white yarn, cast on 4 sts.
Row 1 (RS): Inc 1, knit to last st, inc 1. (6 sts)
Row 2: Inc 1, purl to last st, inc 1. (8 sts)
Repeat the last 2 rows 4 times more. (16 sts)
Work 14 rows in stocking stitch.
Row 31: [K2tog] 8 times. (8 sts)
Row 32: Inc 1, purl to last 2 sts, inc 1, p1. (10 sts)
Row 33: Inc 1, knit to last 2 sts, inc 1, k1. (12 sts)
Row 34: Inc 1, purl to last 2 sts, inc 1, p1. (14 sts)

Right lobe

Row 35: K5, k2tog, transfer the rem 7 sts onto a stitch holder. (6 sts)
Row 36: P2tog, p2, p2tog. (4 sts)
Row 37: K2togtbl, K2tog. (2 sts)
Cast off.

Left lobe

Transfer stitches from stitch holder onto the needle and rejoin yarn.
Row 35: Sl1, k1, psso, k5. (6 sts)
Work as Right lobe rows 36–37.

Beak

Using 3.75mm needles and orange yarn, cast on 2 sts.
Row 1 (RS): [Inc 1] twice. (4 sts)
Row 2: Inc 1, k to the last 2 sts, inc 1, k1. (6 sts)
Repeat the last row 3 times more. (12 sts)
Work 2 rows in garter stitch.
Cast off.

Outer wing (make 2)

Using 3.75mm needles and black yarn, cast on 8 sts.
Row 1 (WS): Purl.
Row 2: Inc 1, k to the last 2 sts, inc 1, k1. (10 sts)
Repeat the last 2 rows once more. (12 sts)
Work 5 rows in stocking stitch.
Row 10: K1, k2togtbl, knit to last 3 sts, k2tog, k1. (10 sts)
Row 11: Purl.
Repeat the last 2 rows 4 times more. (2 sts)
Cast off.

Inner wings (make 2)

Using 3.75mm needles and white yarn, cast on 8 sts.
Work as for Outer wings.

Feet

Using 3.75mm needles and orange yarn, cast on 8 sts.
Row 1 (RS): Inc 1, k to the last 2 sts, inc 1, k1. (10 sts)
Repeat the last row twice more. (14 sts)

Right foot

Row 4: Inc 1, k4, k2tog, transfer the rem 7 sts onto a stitch holder. (8 sts)
Row 5: K1, k2tog, knit to end. (7 sts)
Row 6: K1, k2tog, k1, k2tog, k1. (5 sts)
Cast off.

Left foot

Transfer stitches from stitch holder onto the needle and rejoin yarn.
Row 4: Sl1, k1, psso, k3, inc 1, k1. (7 sts)
Work as Right foot rows 5–6.

Making up

For the body and head, partially sew up side seam, using mattress stitch or backstitch, insert stuffing and complete the seam.
Attach the white bib.
For beak, fold the beak in half and starting from the tip, fold in half, cast-on edge to cast-off edge, and sew together around the outer edge.
For wings, with the stocking stitch side facing outwards, sew the two pieces together, using mattress stitch or backstitch, around the edge.
Draw around the feet onto thin card and stitch the card to the base of the feet.
Using picture as a guide, attach the beak, wings and feet and, using glue, attach the eyes and bowtie.

TO MY SWEETHEART

Materials

- ♥ **A yarn such as:** Patons Fab DK, approx. 68m/25g ball (100% acrylic)
  1 ball in Yellow 2302
  1 ball in Red 2323
  1 ball in Green 2319
- ♥ Pair of 3.75mm needles
- ♥ Tapestry needle
- ♥ Toy filling
- ♥ Two pairs of 8mm wiggle eyes
- ♥ PVA glue or a glue gun

Tension

22 stitches and 26 rows over 10cm stocking stitch.

Rhubarb and Custard (one for each sweet)

Using 3.75mm needles and yellow yarn, cast on 6 sts.
Row 1 (RS): [Inc 1 knitwise] 6 times. (12 sts)
Work 5 rows in stocking stitch.
Row 7: K6 in yellow, break off yellow yarn and join in red, k6.
Work 6 rows in stocking stitch.
Row 14: [K2tog] 6 times. (6 sts)
Cast off.

Lemon Drop (one for each sweet)

Work as for Rhubarb and Custard using only yellow yarn.

Rosie Apple (one for each sweet)

Using 3.75mm needles and red yarn, cast on 3 sts.
Row 1 (RS): [Inc 1, knitwise] 3 times. (6 sts)
Row 2: [Inc 1, purlwise] 6 times. (12 sts)
Row 3: Knit.
Break off red yarn and join in green.
Work 5 rows in stocking stitch.
Break off green yarn and join in red.
Row 9: Knit.
Row 10: [P2tog] 6 times. (6 sts)
Row 11: [K2tog] 3 times. (3 sts)

Break off yarn and thread through stitches on needle.
Draw tight and secure the end.

Making up

For each sweet, partially sew up side seam, using mattress stitch or backstitch, insert stuffing and complete the seam.
Using picture as guide and, using glue, attach eyes to the sweets.

PERFECT MATCH

Materials

- **A yarn such as:** Sirdar Toytime DK Bonus, approx. 70m/25g ball (100% acrylic)
  1 ball in Beige 889
  1 ball in Red 977
- Pair of 3.75mm needles
- Tapestry needle
- Toy filling
- One pair of 5mm wiggle eyes
- PVA glue or a glue gun

Tension

22 stitches and 30 rows over 10cm stocking stitch.

Body and head (make 1 for each match)

Using 3.75mm needles and beige yarn, cast on 5 sts.

Row 1 (WS): Purl.
Row 2: [K1, inc 1] twice, k1. (7 sts)
Work 20 rows in stocking stitch.
Break off beige yarn and join in red.
Work 2 rows in stocking stitch.
Row 25: [Inc 1] 7 times. (14 sts)
Work 3 rows in stocking stitch.
Row 29: K2tog, [k2, k2tog] 3 times. (10 sts)
Row 30: P2tog, [p2, p2tog] twice. (7 sts)
Row 32: K1, [k2tog] 3 times. (4 sts)
Break off yarn and thread through stitches on needle.
Draw tight and secure the end.

Making up

For the body and head, partially sew up side seam, using mattress stitch or backstitch, insert stuffing and complete the seam.

Using picture as guide and, using glue, attach eyes to the head section.

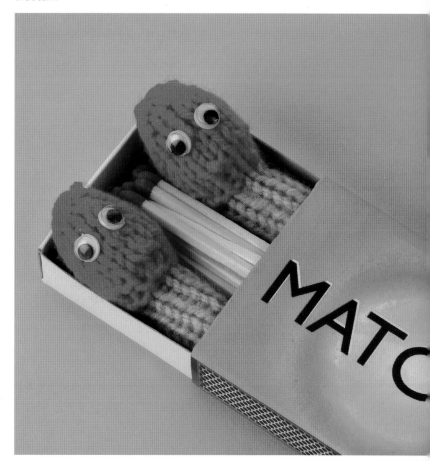

ON OUR ANNIVERSARY

Materials

- **A yarn such as:** Patons Fab DK, approx. 274m/100g ball (100% acrylic)
  1 ball in White 2306
  1 ball in Yellow 2305
- Pair of 3.75mm needles
- Tapestry needle
- Toy filling
- Short length of black yarn
- Four white craft pipe cleaners

Tension

22 stitches and 26 rows over 10cm stocking stitch.

Head and body
(make 1 for each swan)

Using 3.75mm needles and yellow yarn, cast on 3 sts.

Row 1 (WS): Purl.
Row 2: [Inc 1] twice, k1. (5 sts)
Row 3: Inc 1, p2, inc 1, p1. (7 sts)
Row 4: Inc 1, k4, inc 1, k1. (9 sts)
Work 3 rows in stocking stitch.
Break off yellow yarn, join in white yarn.
Row 8: [Inc 1 knitwise] 9 times. (18 sts)
Row 9: Purl.
Row 10: [Inc 1, k2] 6 times. (24 sts)
Work 7 rows in stocking stitch.
Row 18: Inc 1, k9, [k2tog] twice, k8, inc 1, k1.
Row 19: P10, [p2tog] twice, p10. (22 sts)
Row 20: K9, [k2tog] twice, k9. (20 sts)
Row 21: P1, p2tog, p5, [p2tog] twice, p5, p2togtbl, p1. (16 sts)
Row 22: K1, k2togtbl, k3, [k2tog] twice, k3, k2tog, k1. (12 sts)
Row 23: P1, p2tog, p1, [p2tog] twice, p1. p2togtbl, p1. (8 sts)
Work 34 rows in stocking stitch, ending with a purl row.
Row 58: K3, [inc 1] twice, k3. (10 sts)
Row 59: Purl.
Row 60: K4, [inc 1] twice, k4. (12 sts)
Row 61: Purl.
Row 62: K5, [inc 1] twice, k5. (14 sts)
Row 63: Purl.
Row 64: K6, [inc 1] twice, k6. (16 sts)
Row 65: Purl.
Row 66: K7, [inc 1] twice, k7. (18 sts)
Row 67: P8, [inc 1] twice, p8. (20 sts)

Row 68: K9, [inc 1] twice, k9. (22 sts)
Row 69: P10, [inc 1] twice, p10. (24 sts)
Row 70: K11, [inc 1] twice, k11. (26 sts)
Row 71: P12, [inc 1] twice, p12. (28 sts)
Row 72: K13, [inc 1] twice, k13. (30 sts)
Row 73: P14, [inc 1] twice, p14. (32 sts)
Row 74: K15, [inc 1] twice, k15. (34 sts)
Row 75: P16, [inc 1] twice, p16. (36 sts)
Row 76: K17, [inc 1] twice, k17. (38 sts)
Row 77: P18, [inc 1] twice, p18. (40 sts)
Row 78: K19, [inc 1] twice, k19. (42 sts)
Row 79: P20, [inc 1] twice, p20. (44 sts)
Work 2 rows in stocking stitch.
Row 82: K20, [k2tog] twice, k20. (42 sts)
Row 83: Purl.
Row 84: K19, [k2tog] twice, k19. (40 sts)
Row 85: Purl.
Row 86: K18, [k2tog] twice, k18. (38 sts)
Row 87: Purl.
Row 88: K17, [k2tog] twice, k17. (36 sts)
Row 89: Purl.
Row 90: K16, [k2tog] twice, k16. (34 sts)
Row 91: Purl.
Row 92: K15, [k2tog] twice, k15. (32 sts)
Row 93: Purl.
Row 94: K14, [k2tog] twice, k14. (30 sts)
Row 95: Purl.
Row 96: K13, [k2tog] twice, k13. (28 sts)
Row 97: Purl.
Row 98: K1, k2togtbl, k9, [k2tog] twice, k9, k2tog, k1. (24 sts)
Row 99: P1, p2tog, p18, p2togtbl, p1. (22 sts)
Row 100: K1, k2togtbl, k6, [k2tog] twice, k6, k2tog, k1. (18 sts)
Row 101: P1, p2tog, p12, p2togtbl, p1. (16 sts)

Row 102: K1, k2togtbl, k3, [k2tog] twice, k3, k2tog, k1. (12 sts)
Row 103: P1, p2tog, p6, p2togtbl, p1. (10 sts)
Row 104: K1, k2togtbl, k4, k2tog, k1. (8 sts)
Row 105: P1, p2tog, p2, p2togtbl, p1. (6 sts)
Work 2 rows in stocking stitch.
Cast off.

Making up

For the head and body, starting with the beak, partially sew up side seam using mattress stitch or backstitch and insert two pipe cleaners twisted together in the neck section. Insert stuffing in the head, neck and body, but not the tail and complete the seam.

Using picture as guide, embroider eyes using satin stitch.

TOAD-ALLY IN LOVE WITH YOU

Materials

- ♥ **A yarn such as:** Patons Fab DK, approx. 274m/100g ball (100% acrylic)
  1 ball in Green 2341
  Patons Fab DK, approx. 274m/100g (100% acrylic)
  1 ball in Lime 2317
- ♥ Pair of 3.75mm needles
- ♥ Stitch holder
- ♥ Tapestry needle
- ♥ Toy filling
- ♥ Short length of black yarn
- ♥ Two pairs of 15mm wiggle eyes
- ♥ PVA glue or a glue gun

Tension

21 stitches and 29 rows over 10cm stocking stitch.

Body and head (make 2)

Left leg piece

Using 3.75mm needles and lime yarn, cast on 3 sts.
Row 1 (WS): Purl.
Row 2: Knit to last 2 sts, inc 1, k1. (4 sts)
Row 3: Inc 1, purl to end. (5 sts)
Repeat last 2 rows 3 times more. (11 sts)
Row 10: Knit to last 2 sts, inc 1, k1. (12 sts)
Work 4 rows in stocking stitch.
Row 15: Cast off 6 sts, purl to end of row. (6 sts)
Break off lime yarn, join in green yarn.
Work 20 rows in stocking stitch.
Break off yarn and transfer stitches onto a stitch holder.

Right leg piece

Using 3.75mm needles and lime yarn, cast on 3 sts.
Row 1 (WS): Purl.
Row 2: Inc 1, knit to end. (4 sts)
Row 3: Purl to last 2 sts, inc 1, p1. (5 sts)
Repeat last 2 rows 3 times more. (11 sts)
Row 10: Knit to last 2 sts, inc 1, k1. (12 sts)
Work 4 rows in stocking stitch.
Row 15: Cast off 6 sts, purl to end of row. (6 sts)
Break off light green yarn, join in green yarn.
Work 20 rows in stocking stitch.
Break off yarn and transfer stitches onto a stitch holder.

Body

Join the legs by working across the stitches of both legs.
With right sides facing and the needle tip to the right, transfer the stitches from the stitch holder on to a spare needle, then slip the Right leg stitches onto the same needle.
Row 36: Cast on 4 sts, knit across stitches of Right leg, cast on 15 sts, knit across the Left leg. (31 sts)
Row 37: Cast on 4 sts, purl to the end. (35 sts)
Work 4 rows in stocking stitch.
Row 42: Cast off 5 sts, knit to end. (30 sts)
Row 43: Cast off 5 sts, purl to end. (25 sts)
Work 2 rows in stocking stitch.

Row 46: K1, k2togtbl, knit to last 3 sts, k2tog, k1. (23 sts)
Work 3 rows in stocking stitch.
Repeat last 4 rows 8 times more. (15 sts)
Break off green yarn, join in lime yarn.
Work 2 rows in stocking stitch.
Break off lime yarn, join in green yarn.
Row 84: Inc 1, knit to last 2 sts, inc 1, k1. (17 sts)
Work 3 rows in stocking stitch.
Row 88: Inc 1, knit to last 2 sts, inc 1, k1. (19 sts)
Row 89: Purl.
Repeat last 4 rows once more. (21 sts)

Right eye

Row 90: K6, transfer the rem 15 sts onto a stitch holder. (6 sts)
Row 91: P1, p2tog, p2. (5 sts)
Row 92: K2, k2tog, k1. (4 sts)
Row 93: P1, p2tog, p1. (3 sts)
Row 94: Sl1, k2tog, psso.
Fasten off.

Left eye

Transfer stitches from stitch holder onto the needle and rejoin yarn.
Row 90: Cast off 9 sts, knit to end. (6 sts)
Row 91: P3, p2tog, p1. (5 sts)
Row 92: K1, k2tog, k2. (4 sts)
Row 93: P1, p2tog, p1. (3 sts)
Row 94: Sl1, k2tog, psso.
Fasten off.

Arms (make 4)

Using 3.75mm needles and green yarn,
cast on 4 sts.

Row 1. Knit.

Row 2: Purl.

Row 3: Inc 1, knit to last 2 sts, inc 1, k1.
  (6 sts)

Work 13 rows in stocking stitch.

Break off green yarn, join in lime yarn.

Row 17. Knit.

Row 18: Inc 1, purl to last 2 sts, inc 1, k1.
  (8 sts)

Row 19: Inc 1, knit to last 2 sts, inc 1, k1.
  (10 sts)

Work 3 rows in stocking stitch.

Row 23: K1, sl1, k1, psso, k4, k2tog, k1.
  (8 sts)

Row 24: P1, p2togtbl, p2, p2tog, p1.
  (6 sts)

Row 25: K1, sl1, k1, psso, k2tog, k1.
  (4 sts)

Row 26: P2togtbl, p2tog. (2 sts)

Work 2 rows in stocking stitch.

Cast off.

Making up

For the body and head, partially sew
the two pieces together using mattress
stitch or backstitch, insert stuffing and
complete the seam. Repeat with each
arm.

Using picture as guide, embroider the
mouth using backstitch and, using glue,
attach eyes to the head section.

YOU'RE TWEET

Materials

- ❤ **A yarn such as:** any self-striping fluffy yarn (for a stripey chick) or Sirdar Funky Fur DK, approx. 90m/50g ball (100% polyester) 1 ball in White 512
  Sirdar Calico DK, approx. 158m/50g ball (60% cotton, 40% acrylic) 1 ball in Yellow 733
  Sirdar Toytime DK Bonus, approx. 70m/25g ball (100% acrylic) 1 ball in Red 977
- ❤ Pair of 3.75mm needles
- ❤ Stitch holder
- ❤ Tapestry needle
- ❤ Toy filling
- ❤ Short length of black yarn

Tension

24 stitches and 30 rows over 10cm stocking stitch.

Body and head
(make 1 for each chick)

Using 3.75mm needles and fluffy yarn, cast on 7 sts.
Row 1 (RS): [Inc 1, knitwise] 7 times. (14 sts)
Row 2: Purl.
Row 3: [K1, inc 1] 14 times. (28 sts)
Work 13 rows in stocking stitch.
Row 17: [K2tog] 14 times. (14 sts)
Row 18: Purl.
Row 19: [K1, inc 1] 7 times. (21 sts)
Work 12 rows in stocking stitch.
Row 32: P1, [p2tog] 10 times. (11 sts)

Row 33: [K2tog] 5 times, k1. (6 sts)
Break off yarn and thread through stitches on needle.
Draw tight and secure the end.

Base

Using 3.75mm needles and fluffy yarn, cast on 8 sts.
Row 1 and each alternate row (WS): Purl.
Row 2: [Inc 1] 8 times (16 sts)
Row 4: [Inc 1, k1] 8 times. (24 sts)
Row 6: [Inc 1, k2] 8 times. (32 sts)
Row 8: [Inc 1, k3] 8 times. (40 sts)
Row 9: Purl.
Cast off.

Wings
(make 2 for each chick)

Using 3.75mm needles and fluffy yarn, cast on 3 sts.
Row 1 (WS): Purl.
Row 2: [Inc 1] twice, k1. (5 sts)
Row 3: Purl.
Row 4: Inc 1, k2, inc 1, k1. (7 sts)
Work 12 rows in stocking stitch.
Row 17: P1, p2tog, p1, p2togtbl, p1. (5 sts)
Row 18: Knit.
Row 19: P2tog, p1, p2togtbl. (3 sts)
Row 18: Knit.
Cast off.

Beak (make 1 for each chick)

Using 3.75mm needles and yellow yarn, cast on 3 sts.
Row 1 (RS): [Inc 1] twice, k1. (5 sts)
Work 4 rows in stocking stitch.

Row 6: P2tog, p1, p2togtbl. (3 sts)
Cast off.

Feet (make 2 for each chick)

Using 3.75mm needles and yellow yarn, cast on 3 sts.
Row 1 (WS): [Inc 1] twice, p1. (5 sts)
Work 4 rows in stocking stitch.
Row 6: K1, [k2tog, yo] twice. (5 sts)
Work 4 rows in stocking stitch.
Row 11: P2tog, p1, p2togtbl. (3 sts)
Cast off.

Heart (make 2)

Using 3.75mm needles and red yarn, cast on 4 sts.
Row 1 (RS): [Inc 1, k1] twice. (6 sts)
Row 2: Inc 1, purl to last 2 sts, inc 1, p1. (8 sts)
Repeat last 2 rows 3 times more. (14 sts)
Work 3 rows in stocking stitch.
Row 12: P1, p2tog, p6, p2togtbl, p1. (12 sts)

Right lobe

Row 13: K1, sl1, k1, psso, k1, k2tog, transfer the rem 6 sts onto a stitch holder. (4 sts)
Row 14: P2tog, p2togtbl. (2 sts)
Cast off.

Left lobe

Transfer stitches from stitch holder onto the needle and rejoin yarn.
Row 13: K1, sl1, k1, psso, k1, k2tog. (4 sts)
Row 14: P2tog, p2togtbl. (2 sts)
Cast off.

Making up

For the body and head, partially sew up side seam, using mattress stitch or backstitch, insert stuffing and complete the seam.

Stitch the base to the bottom of the body.

For the feet, wings and beak, with the stocking stitch side facing outwards, fold in half, cast-on edge to cast-off edge, and sew together around the outer edge.

Using picture as guide and matching yarn, attach the feet, wings and beak and embroider the eyes using satin stitch.

For the heart, partially sew around the edge, insert stuffing and complete the seam.

OWL ALWAYS LOVE YOU

Materials

- **A yarn such as:** Sirdar Classics DK Bonus, approx. 280m/100g ball (100% acrylic)
  1 ball in Beige tweed 596
  Sirdar Toytime DK Bonus, approx. 70m/25g ball (100% acrylic)
  1 ball in Yellow 978
- Pair of 3.75mm needles
- Tapestry needle
- Toy filling
- Two pairs of 20mm wiggle eyes
- PVA glue or a glue gun
- Two orange craft pipe cleaners

Tension

22 stitches and 26 rows over 10cm stocking stitch.

Body and head

Using 3.75mm needles and beige tweed yarn, cast on 11 sts.
Row 1 (RS): [Inc 1, knitwise] 11 times. (22 sts)
Row 2: Purl.
Row 3: [Inc 1, k1] 11 times. (33 sts)
Row 4: Purl.
Row 5: [Inc 1, k2] 11 times. (44 sts)
Work 13 rows in stocking stitch.
Row 19: [Inc 1, k1] 22 times. (66 sts)
Work 13 rows in stocking stitch.
Row 33: K3, [k2tog, k4] 10 times, k2tog, k1. (55 sts)
Row 34: P1, [p2tog, p3] 10 times, p2tog, p2. (44 sts)
Row 35: K1, [k2tog, k2] 10 times, k2tog, k1. (33 sts)
Row 36: [P1, p2tog] 11 times. (22 sts)
Row 37: [K2tog] 11 times. (11 sts)
Row 38: P1, [p2tog] 5 times. (6 sts)
Break off yarn and thread through stitches on needle.
Draw tight and secure the end.

Base

Using 3.75mm needles and beige tweed yarn, cast on 8 sts.
Row 1 and each alternate row (WS): Purl.
Row 2: [Inc 1] 8 times (16 sts)
Row 4: [Inc 1, k1] 8 times. (24 sts)
Row 6: [Inc 1, k2] 8 times. (32 sts)
Row 8: [Inc 1, k3] 8 times. (40 sts)
Row 9: Purl.
Cast off.

Wings (make 2)

Using 3.75mm needles and beige tweed yarn, cast on 3 sts.
Row 1 (RS): Inc 1, knit to last 2 sts, inc 1, k1. (5 sts)
Row 2: Purl.
Repeat last 2 rows 3 times more. (6 sts)
Work 20 rows in stocking stitch.
Row 29: K1, k2togtbl, knit to last 2 sts, k2tog, k1. (9 sts)
Row 30: Purl.
Repeat last 2 rows twice more. (5 sts)
Row 35: K1, k2togtbl, k2tog. (3 sts)
Row 36: Purl.
Cast off.

Ears (make 2)

Using 3.75mm needles and beige tweed yarn, cast on 5 sts.
Work 2 rows in garter stitch.
Row 3: K2togtbl, k1, k2tog. (3 sts)
Row 4: K2togtbl, k1. (2 sts)
Row 5: K2togtbl. (1 st)
Cast off.

Beak

Using 3.75mm needles and yellow yarn, cast on 2 sts.
Row 1 (RS): [Inc 1, knitwise] twice. (4 sts)
Row 2: Inc 1, purl to last 2 sts, inc 1, p1. (6 sts)
Row 3: Inc 1, knit to last 2 sts, inc 1, k1. (8 sts)
Repeat last 2 rows 3 times more. (16 sts)
Cast off.

Making up

For the body and head, partially sew up side seam, using mattress stitch or backstitch, insert stuffing and complete the seam.

Stitch the base to the bottom of the body.

For the wings, with the reverse stocking stitch side facing outwards, fold in half, cast-on edge to cast-off edge, and sew together around the outer edge.

With the stocking stitch side facing outwards, fold the beak in half and starting from the tip, sew along half of the edge.

Using picture as guide and matching yarn, attach the wings, beak and ears and, using glue, attach the eyes.

Using the pipe cleaners, make two feet and attach them to the body.

TO THE ONE I LOVE

Materials

- ♥ **A yarn such as:** Patons Fab DK, approx. 274m/100g ball (100% acrylic)
  1 ball in Red 2323
- ♥ Pair of 3.75mm needles
- ♥ Stitch holder
- ♥ Tapestry needle
- ♥ Toy filling
- ♥ Short length of cream yarn
- ♥ One pair of 10mm wiggle eyes
- ♥ PVA glue or a glue gun
- ♥ Two thick red craft pipe cleaners

Tension

22 stitches and 30 rows over 10cm stocking stitch.

Body and head (make 2)

Using 3.75mm needles and red yarn, cast on 4 sts.
Row 1 (RS): Inc 1, knit to last 2 sts, inc 1, k1. (6 sts)
Row 2: Inc 1, purl to last 2 sts, inc 1, k1. (8 sts)
Repeat last 2 rows 13 times more. (34 sts)
Work 8 rows in stocking stitch.

Row 24: P1, p2tog, purl to last 3 sts, p2togtbl, p1. (32 sts)

Right lobe

Row 25: K1, sl1, k1, psso, k10, k2tog, k1, transfer the rem 16 sts onto a stitch holder. (14 sts)
**Row 26: P1, p2tog, purl to last 3 sts, p2togtbl, p1. (12 sts)
Row 27: K1, sl1, k1, psso, knit to last 3 sts, k2tog, k1. (10 sts)
Repeat last 2 rows once more. (6 sts)
Row 30: P1, p2tog, p2togtbl, p1. (4 sts)
Cast off.

Left lobe

Transfer stitches from stitch holder onto the needle and rejoin yarn.
Row 25: K1, sl1, k1, psso, k10, k2tog, k1. (14 sts)
Continue from ** on Right lobe.

Making up

For the body and head, sew the two pieces together using mattress stitch or backstitch, insert stuffing and complete the seam.
Using picture as guide, embroider the mouth using backstitch and, using glue, attach the eyes.
Using the pipe cleaners, make two arms and two legs; then attach them to the base of the heart.

CONGRATULATIONS!

Materials

- ♥ **A yarn such as:** Patons Fab DK, approx. 274m/100g ball (100% acrylic)
  1 ball in Green 2341
  Patons Fab DK, approx. 68m/25g ball (100% acrylic)
  1 ball in Gold 2305
- ♥ Pair of 3.75mm needles
- ♥ Tapestry needle
- ♥ Toy filling
- ♥ Paper label
- ♥ PVA glue or a glue gun

Tension

22 stitches and 30 rows over 10cm stocking stitch.

Body and neck

Using 3.75mm needles and green yarn, cast on 12 sts.

Row 1 (WS): Purl.
Row 2: [Inc 1, knitwise] 12 times. (24 sts)
Row 3: Purl.
Row 4: [Inc 1, knitwise] 24 times. (48 sts)
Work 25 rows in stocking stitch.
Row 30: K5, [k2tog, k10] 3 times, k5, k2tog. (44 sts)
Row 31: Purl.
Row 32: K5, [k2tog, k9] 3 times, k4, k2tog. (40 sts)
Row 33: Purl.
Row 34: K4, [k2tog, k8] 3 times, k4, k2tog. (36 sts)
Row 35: Purl.

Row 36: K4, [k2tog, k7] 3 times, k3, k2tog. (32 sts)

Row 37: Purl.

Row 38: K3, [k2tog, k6] 3 times, k3, k2tog. (28 sts)

Row 39: Purl.

Row 40: K3, [k2tog, k5] 3 times, k2, k2tog. (24 sts)

Work 13 rows in stocking stitch.

Cast off.

Base

Using 3.75mm needles and green yarn, cast on 8 sts.

Row 1 and each alternate row (WS): Purl.

Row 2: [Inc 1] 8 times (16 sts)

Row 4: [Inc 1, k1] 8 times. (24 sts)

Row 6: K1, [inc 1, k2] 7 times, inc 1, k1. (32 sts)

Row 8: K1, [inc 1, k3] 7 times, inc 1, k2. (40 sts)

Row 9: Purl.

Cast off.

Cork

Using 3.75mm needles and gold yarn, cast on 6 sts.

Row 1 (RS): [Inc 1, knitwise] 6 times. (12 sts)

Row 2: Purl.

Row 3: [Inc 1] 12 times. (24 sts)

Work 7 rows in stocking stitch.

Row 11: [Inc 1, k1] 12 times. (36 sts)

Work 7 rows in stocking stitch.

Row 19: K2, [k2tog, k4] 5 times, k2tog, k2. (30 sts)

Row 20: Purl.

Row 21: K2, [k2tog, k3] 5 times, k2tog, k1. (24 sts)

Row 22: Purl.

Row 23: K1, [k2tog, k2] 5 times, k2tog, k1. (18 sts)

Row 24: Purl.

Row 25: K1, [k2tog, k1] 5 times, k2tog. (12 sts)

Row 26: Purl.

Row 27: [K2tog] 6 times. (6 sts)

Row 28: Purl.

Break off yarn and thread through stitches on needle.

Draw tight and secure the end.

Making up

For the body and neck, partially sew up side seam, using mattress stitch or backstitch, insert stuffing and complete the seam.

Stitch the base to the bottom of the body.

Leave the top of the bottle open and let the stuffing escape slightly.

For the cork, partially sew up side seam, insert stuffing and complete the seam.

Using glue, paste paper label to the body.

JUST MARRIED

Materials

- ♥ **A yarn such as:** Patons Fab DK, approx. 274m/100g ball (100% acrylic)
  2 balls in White 2306
- ♥ Pair of 3.75mm needles
- ♥ Tapestry needle
- ♥ Toy filling
- ♥ Sewing needle and white thread
- ♥ Nine small fabric roses
- ♥ Nine medium-sized fabric rose bunches with ribbon and pearl-bead chain
- ♥ Nine large fabric rose bunches with ribbon and pearl-bead chain

Tension

21 stitches and 30 rows over 10cm stocking stitch.

BOTTOM CAKE TIER

Cake top

Using 3.75mm needles and white yarn, cast on 8 sts.

Row 1 and each alternate row (WS): Purl.

Row 2: [Inc 1] 8 times. (16 sts)

Row 4: [Inc 1, k1] 8 times. (24 sts)

Row 6: K1, [inc 1, k2] 7 times, inc 1, k1. (32 sts)

Row 8: K1, [inc 1, k3] 7 times, inc 1, k2. (40 sts)

Row 10: K2, [inc 1, k4] 7 times, inc 1, k2. (48 sts)

Row 12: K2, [inc 1, k5] 7 times, inc 1, k3.
(56 sts)
Row 14: K3, [inc 1, k6] 7 times, inc 1, k3.
(64 sts)
Row 16: K3, [inc 1, k7] 7 times, inc 1, k4.
(72 sts)
Row 18: K4, [inc 1, k8] 7 times, inc 1, k4.
(80sts)
Row 20: K4, [inc 1, k9] 7 times, inc 1, k5.
(88 sts)
Row 22: K5, [inc 1, k10] 7 times, inc 1, k5.
(96 sts)
Row 24: K5, [inc 1, k11] 7 times, inc 1, k6.
(104 sts)
Row 26: K6, [inc 1, k12] 7 times, inc 1, k6.
(112 sts)
Row 28: K6, [inc 1, k13] 7 times, inc 1, k7.
(120 sts)
Row 30: K7, [inc 1, k14] 7 times, inc 1, k7.
(128 sts)
Row 31: Purl.
Cast off: [Cast on 2 sts, cast off 4 sts]
repeat to end.

Cake bottom

Work as Cake top.

Side of cake

Using 3.75mm needles and white yarn,
cast on 136 sts.
Row 1 (RS): K17, [p1, k16] 7 times.
Row 2: P15, [k1, p1, k1] 7 times.
Row 3: K15, [p1, k3, p1, k14] 7 times.
Row 4: P13, [k1, p5, k1, p14] 7 times.
Row 5: K13, [p1, k7, p1, k12] 7 times.
Row 6: P11, [k1, p9, k1, p12] 7 times.
Row 7: K11, [p1, k11, p1, k10] 7 times.
Row 8: P9, [k1, p13, k1, p10] 7 times.
Row 9: K9, [p1, k15, p1, k8] 7 times.

Row 10: P7, [k1, p17, k1, p8] 7 times.
Row 11: K7, [p1, k19, p1, k6] 7 times.
Row 12: P5, [k1, p21, k1, p5] 7 times.
Row 13: K5, [p1, k23, p1, k4] 7 times.
Row 14: P3, [k1, p25, k1, p4] 7 times.
Row 15: K3, [p1, k27, p1, k2] 7 times.
Row 16: P1, [k1, p29, k1, p2] 7 times.
Row 17: K1, [p1, k31, p1] 7 times.
Row 18: [P33, k1] 4 times.
Cast off

MIDDLE CAKE TIER

Cake top

Work rows 1–26 Bottom cake tier,
Cake top.
Cast off as Bottom cake tier, Cake top.

Cake bottom

Work rows as Cake top.

Side of cake

Using 3.75mm needles and white yarn,
cast on 102 sts.
Work rows 1–26 Bottom cake tier, Side
of cake.

TOP TIER

Cake top

Work rows 1–18 Bottom cake tier, Cake
top.
Cast off as Bottom cake tier, Cake top.

Cake bottom

Work rows as Cake top.

Side of cake

Using 3.75mm needles and white yarn,
cast on 78 sts.
Work rows 1–26 Bottom cake tier, Side
of cake.

Making up

For the Bottom cake tier, sew up side
seams, using mattress stitch or
backstitch, attach top, insert stuffing
and attach bottom with the reverse
stocking stitch side facing outwards.
Repeat for the Middle cake tier and the
Top cake tier.
Using picture as guide and using sewing
thread, attach the roses with small
stitches.

WEDDING DREAMS

Materials

- ♥ **A yarn such as:** Sirdar Classics DK Bonus, approx. 280m/100g ball (100% acrylic)
  1 ball in Copper 843
  Patons Fab DK, approx. 68m/25g ball (100% acrylic)
  1 ball in White 2306
- ♥ Pair of 3.75mm needles
- ♥ Stitch holder
- ♥ Tapestry needle
- ♥ A pair of compasses
- ♥ Scalpel
- ♥ Cutting mat
- ♥ Toy filling
- ♥ Short lengths of cream and red yarn
- ♥ Two small fabric roses
- ♥ Three large fabric rose with stems
- ♥ Sewing needle and matching thread
- ♥ Thin black card for hat
- ♥ PVA glue or a glue gun

Tension

22 stitches and 30 rows over 10cm stocking stitch.

GINGERBREAD MALE

Body and head (make 2)
Left leg piece
Using 3.75mm needles and copper yarn, cast on 4 sts.
Row 1 (WS): Purl.
Row 2: Inc 1, knit to last 2 sts, inc 1, k1. (6 sts)

Row 3: Purl.
Row 4: Inc 1, k2, k2tog, k1. (6 sts)
Row 5: Purl.
Repeat last 2 rows 5 times more.
Break off yarn and transfer stitches onto a stitch holder.

Right leg piece
Using 3.75mm needles and copper yarn, cast on 4 sts.
Row 1 (WS): Purl.
Row 2: Inc 1, knit to last 2 sts, inc 1, k1. (6 sts)
Row 3: Purl.
Row 4: K1, K2togtbl, k1, inc 1, k1. (6 sts)
Row 5: Purl.
Repeat last 2 rows 5 times more.

Body
Join the legs by working across the stitches of both legs.
With right sides facing and the needle tip to the right, transfer the stitches from the stitch holder on to a spare needle, then slip the Right leg onto the same needle.
Row 16: K5, k2tog (last st from Right leg and first st of Left leg), cont to work across the Left leg stitches, k5. (11 sts)
**Work 9 rows in stocking stitch, ending with a purl row.

Arms
Row 26: Cast on 8 sts, knit to end. (19 sts)

Row 27: Cast on 8 sts, purl to end. (27 sts)
Work 2 rows in stocking stitch.
Row 30: Cast on 8 sts, knit to end. (19 sts)
Row 31: Cast on 8 sts, purl to end. (11 sts)
Row 32: K1, k2togtbl, knit to last 3 sts, k2tog, k1. (9 sts)
Row 33: P1, P2tog, purl to last 3 sts, p2togtbl, p1. (7 sts)
Row 34: Knit.

Head
Row 35: Inc 1, purl to last 2 sts, inc 1, k1. (9 sts)
Row 36: Inc 1, knit to last 2 sts, inc 1, k1. (11 sts)

Work 3 rows in stocking stitch.
Row 39: K1, k2tog, knit to last 3 sts,
    k2tog, k1. (9 sts)
Row 40: Purl.
Repeat last 2 rows 3 times more. (3 sts)
Cast off.

Making up

For the body and head, partially sew the
two pieces together using mattress
stitch or backstitch, insert stuffing and
complete the seam.
Using picture as guide, embroider the
mouth using chain stitch, the eyes and
buttons using satin stitch.
Using sewing thread, stitch a small rose
to the chest.

Hat

Using the thin black card.
For the brim: Draw a circle and cut out a
circle 6.5cm in diameter.
For the crown: Cut a strip 3.5cm x 16cm,
curl into a cylinder and glue the short
edge with a 5mm overlap. Draw a circle
5.5cm in diameter with an inner circle
with the same centre point with a
diameter of 5cm. Cut out the outer circle
and snip the edge of the disc up to the
line marking the inner circle. Crease the
snip edge along the line of the inner
circle. Paste glue over the snipped margin
and place the disc just inside one edge of
the cylinder, so that the disc aligns with
the edge of the cylinder. Draw a second
circle 5.5cm in diameter and repeat with
the other end of the cylinder.Paste glue
on the disc at one end of the cylinder and
glue to the brim.Glue the hat to the head.

GINGERBREAD FEMALE

Body and head (make 2)
Skirt
Using 3.75mm needles and copper yarn,
cast on 35 sts.
Row 1 (WS): Purl.
Row 2: K4, [sl1, k2tog, psso, k3] 5 times,
    k1. (25 sts)
Row 3: Purl.
Row 4: K3, [sl1, k2tog, psso, k1] 5 times,
    k2. (15 sts)
Work 3 rows in stocking stitch.
Row 8: K1, k2togtbl, knit to last 3 sts,
    k2tog, k1. (13 sts)
Row 9: Purl.
Row 10: K1, k2togtbl, knit to last 3 sts,
    k2tog, k1. (11 sts)
Continue from ** on Gingerbread Male
Body and Head.

Veil

Using 3.75mm needles and white yarn,
cast on 35 sts.
Work 40 rows in garter stitch.
Row 41: K4, [sl1, k2tog, psso, k3]
    5 times, k1. (25 sts)
Row 42: Purl.
Row 43: K3, [sl1, k2tog, psso, k1] 5 times,
    k2. (15 sts)
Row 44: Purl.
Row 45: K2, [sl1, k2tog, psso] 4 times,
    k1. (11 sts)
Row 44: Purl.
Break off yarn and thread through
stitches on needle.
Draw tight and secure the end.
Fold the cast-off edge corner to corner
and sew the top edge together.

Making up

For the body and head, partially sew
the two pieces together using mattress
stitch or backstitch, insert stuffing and
complete the seam.
Using picture as guide and glue attach
eyes to the head section.
Using picture as guide, embroider the
mouth using chain stitch, the eyes and
buttons using satin stitch.
Using sewing thread, attach the veil to
the head and embellish with a small
fabric rose.
Make a bouquet of large fabric roses,
using sewing thread, position the arms
and secure the bouquet and arms in
position with small stitches.

KNITTING BASICS

WORKING FROM A PATTERN

Before starting any pattern, always read it through. This will give you an idea of how the design is structured and the techniques that are involved. Each pattern includes the following basic elements:

Materials

This section gives a list of materials required, including the amount of yarn, the sizes of needles and extras.

Abbreviations

Knitting instructions are normally given in an abbreviated form, which saves valuable space. In this book the abbreviations are listed on page 48.

Project instructions

Before starting to knit, read the instructions carefully to understand the abbreviations used, how the design is structured and in which order each piece is worked. However, there may be some parts of the pattern that only become clear when you are knitting them, so do not assume that you are being slow or that the pattern is wrong.

Tension (gauge) and selecting correct needle size

Tension (gauge) can differ quite dramatically between knitters. This is because of the way that the needles and the yarn are held. So if your tension (gauge) does not match that stated in the pattern, you should change your needle size following this simple rule:

❤ If your knitting is too loose, your tension (gauge) will read that you have fewer stitches and rows than the given tension (gauge), and you will need to change to a smaller needle to make the stitch size smaller.

❤ If your knitting is too tight, your tension (gauge) will read that you have more stitches and rows than the given tension (gauge), and you will need to change to a thicker needle to make the stitch size bigger.

Making up

The Making up section in each project will tell you how to join the knitted pieces together. Always follow the recommended sequence.

KNITTING A TENSION SWATCH

No matter how excited you are about a new knitting project and how annoying it seems to have to spend time knitting a tension swatch before you start, please do take the time, as it will not be wasted.

Use the same needles, yarn and stitch pattern as those that will be used for the main work and knit a sample at least 12.5cm (5in) square. Smooth out the finished piece on a flat surface, but do not stretch it.

To check the stitch tension, place a ruler horizontally on the sample, measure 10cm (4in) across and mark with a pin at each end. Count the number of stitches between the pins. To check the row tension, place a ruler vertically on the sample, measure 10cm (4in) and mark with pins. Count the number of rows between the pins. If the number of stitches and rows is greater then specified in the pattern, make a new swatch using larger needles; if it is less, make a new swatch using smaller needles.

MAKING A SLIP KNOT

A slip knot is the basis of all casting-on techniques and is therefore the starting point for almost everything you do in knitting.

1 Wind the yarn around two fingers twice, as shown. Insert a knitting needle through the first (front) strand and under the second (back) one.

2 Using the needle, pull the back strand through the front one to form a loop. Holding the loose ends of the yarn with your left hand, pull the needle upwards, thus tightening the knot.

CASTING ON

Casting on is the term used for making a row of stitches to be used as a foundation for your knitting.

1 Place the slip knot on the needle, leaving a long tail, and hold the needle in your right hand.

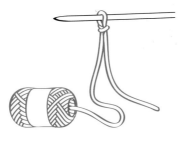

2 * Wind the loose end of the yarn around your thumb from front to back. Place the ball end of the yarn over your left forefinger.

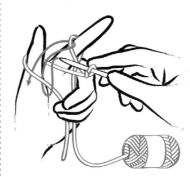

3 Insert the point of the needle under the loop on your thumb. With your right index finger, take the ball end of the yarn over the point of the needle.

4 Pull a loop through to form the first stitch. Remove your left thumb from the yarn. Pull the loose end to secure the stitch. Repeat from * until the required number of stitches has been cast on.

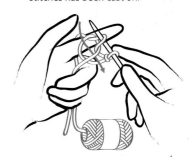

THE BASIC STITCHES

The knit and purl stitches form the basis of all knitted fabrics. The knit stitch is the easiest to learn. Once you have mastered this, you can move on to the purl stitch.

Knit stitch

1 Hold the needle with the cast-on stitches in your left hand, with the loose yarn at the back of the work. Insert the right-hand needle from left to right through the front of the first stitch on the left-hand needle.

2 Wrap the yarn from left to right over the point of the right-hand needle.

3 Draw the yarn through the stitch, thus forming a new stitch on the right-hand needle.

4 Slip the original stitch off the left-hand needle, keeping the new stitch on the right-hand needle. To knit a row, repeat steps 1 to 4 until all the stitches have been transferred from the left-hand needle to the right-hand needle.

Purl stitch

1 Hold the needle with the stitches in your left hand, with the loose yarn at the front of the work. Insert the right-hand needle from right to left into the front of the first stitch on the left-hand needle.

2 Wrap the yarn from right to left, up and over the point of the right-hand needle.

3 Draw the yarn through the stitch, thus forming a new stitch on the right-hand needle.

4 Slip the original stitch off the left-hand needle, keeping the new stitch on the right-hand needle. To purl a row, repeat steps 1–4 until all the stitches have been transferred from the left-hand needle to the right-hand needle.

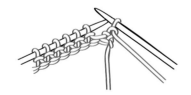

INCREASING AND DECREASING

Many projects will require some shaping. This is achieved by increasing or decreasing the number of stitches you are working.

Increasing

The simplest method of increasing one stitch is to work into the front and back of the same stitch. On a knit row, knit into the front of the stitch to be increased into; then, before slipping it off the needle, place the right-hand needle behind the left-hand one and knit again into the back of it (inc). Slip the original stitch off the left-hand needle. On a purl row, purl into the front of the stitch to be increased into; then, before slipping it off the needle, purl again into the back of it. Slip the original stitch off the left-hand needle.

Decreasing

The simplest method of decreasing one stitch is to work two stitches together. On a knit row, insert the right-hand needle from left to right through two stitches instead of one, then knit them together as one stitch. This is called knit two together (k2tog). On a purl row, insert the right-hand needle from right to left through two stitches instead of one, then purl them together as one stitch. This is called purl two together (p2tog).

CASTING OFF

This is the most commonly used method of securing stitches once you have finished a piece of knitting. The cast-off edge should have the same 'give' or elasticity as the fabric, and you should cast off in the stitch used for the main fabric unless the pattern directs otherwise.

Knitwise

Knit two stitches. * Using the point of the left-hand needle, lift the first stitch on the right-hand needle over the second, then drop it off the needle. Knit the next stitch and repeat from * until all stitches have been worked off the left-hand needle and only one stitch remains on the right-hand needle. Cut the yarn, leaving enough to sew in the end, thread the end through the stitch, then slip it off the needle. Draw the yarn up firmly to fasten off.

Purlwise

Purl two stitches. * Using the point of the left-hand needle, lift the first stitch on the right-hand needle over the second and drop it off the needle. Purl the next stitch and repeat from * until all the stitches have been worked off the left-hand needle and only one stitch remains on the right-hand needle. Secure the last stitch as described in casting off knitwise.

SEWING BASICS

FINISHING TECHNIQUES

You may have finished knitting but there is one crucial step still to come, the sewing up of the seams. It is tempting to start this as soon as you cast off the last stitch but a word of caution: make sure that you have good light and plenty of time to complete the task.

MATTRESS STITCH (SIDE EDGES)

This stitch makes an almost invisible seam on the knit side of stocking stitch. Thread a tapestry needle with yarn and position the pieces side by side, right sides facing.

1   Working from the bottom of the seam to the top, come up from back to front at the base of the seam, to the left of the first stitch in from the edge on the left-hand side, and leave a 10cm tail of yarn. Take the needle across to the right-hand piece, to the right of the first stitch, pass the needle under the first two of the horizontal bars that divide the columns of stitches above the cast-on.

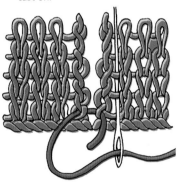

2   Take the needle across to the left-hand piece, insert the needle down where it last emerged on the left-hand edge, pass the needle under two of the horizontal bars that divide the columns of stitches. Take the needle across to the right-hand piece, insert the needle down through the fabric where it last emerged on the right-hand edge, pass the needle under the first two of the horizontal bars that divide the columns of stitches above the cast-on. Repeat step 2 until the seam has been closed.

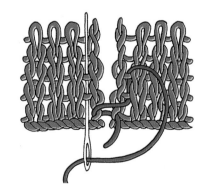

MATTRESS STITCH (TOP AND BOTTOM EDGES)

Thread a tapestry needle with yarn and position the pieces top and bottom, right sides facing outermost. Working left to right, come up from back to front through the centre of first stitch on the right edge of the seam and leave a 10cm tail of yarn. Take the needle across to the top piece, pass the needle under the two loops of the stitch above, then go down again, through the fabric, where the needle emerged on the lower piece. Repeat with the next stitch to the left.

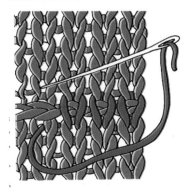

SATIN STITCH

Work a series of short straight stitches, parallel to each other, to create a pad of stitches.

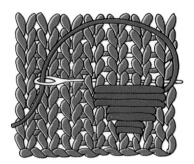

INSERTING STUFFING

As with all soft toys, how you stuff your doll will directly affect the finished appearance. It is important to stuff firmly, but without stretching the knitting out of place. Always stuff down the extremities, such as the legs and arms, first and mould into shape as you go along. The amount of stuffing needed for each doll depends on the knitting tension and individual taste.

CONVERSIONS

Needle sizes

This table gives you the equivalent sizes across all three systems of sizing needles.

Metric	US	old UK/Canadian
25	50	–
19	35	–
15	19	–
10	15	000
9	13	00
8	11	0
7.5	11	1
7	10½	2
6.5	10½	3
6	10	4
5.5	9	5
5	8	6
4.5	7	7
4	6	8
3.75	5	9
3.5	4	–
3.25	3	10
3	⅔	11
2.75	2	12
2.25	1	13
2	0	14
1.75	00	–
1.5	000	–

Weights and lengths

grams = ounces x 28.35
ounces = grams x 0.0352
centimetres = inches x 2.54
inches = centimetres x 0.3937
metres = yards x 1.0936
yards = metres x 0.9144

ABBREVIATIONS

approx	approximately
alt	alternate
beg	beginning
cm	centimetre
dec	decrease
in	inch(es)
inc	increase
k	knit
k2tog	knit two together
k3tog	knit three together
LH	left hand
m1	make one
mm	millimetre(s)
MB	Make bobble: Knit into front, back, and front of next st, turn and k3, turn and p3, turn and k3, turn and slip 1, k2tog, psso.
MC	Main colour
oz	ounce(s)
p	purl
p2tog	purl two together
rem	remaining
psso	pass slipped stitch over
rep	repeat
RH	right hand
RS	right side
sl	slip
ssk	slip slip knit
st st	stocking stitch
st(s)	stitch(es)
tbl	through back loop
tog	together
WS	wrong side
yd	yard
yfwd	yarn forward

AUTHOR'S AKNOWLEDGMENTS

I hope you will have as much fun knitting all the wonderful characters in this book as I had creating them! When I started knitting them for the Knit & Purl greetings card range I never dreamt that it would lead to a pattern book.

I would like to thank everyone at Mint Publishing for their inspiration, patience and support in the development of the characters. Thank you also to my family, especially Alan, for putting up with my many attempts at some of these characters, and their diplomacy when the finished item didn't really look like it should do, and the gentle persuasion to try again.

Last but not least thank you to Anova Books, especially Amy and Katie, for giving me this opportunity and guiding me through such a daunting project. I never thought when my Grandma taught to knit all those years ago that it would lead to this!

Debbie Harrold